PERFECT PUT-DOWNS and INSTANT INSULTS

by

JOSEPH ROSENBLOOM

Pictures by Sanford Hoffman

 Sterling Publishing Co., Inc.   New York

To Danielle Backerman

Library of Congress Cataloging-in-Publication Data

Rosenbloom, Joseph.
  Perfect put-downs & instant insults / Joseph Rosenbloom : drawings
by Sandy Hoffman.
    p. cm.
  Includes index.
  Summary: A collection of hundreds of humorous insults, from one-
liners to knock-knock jokes, illustrated with cartoon drawings.
  1. Invective—Juvenile humor.   2. Wit and humor, Juvenile.
[1. Invective—Wit and humor. 2. Wit and humor.] I. Hoffman,
Sanford, ill.   II. Title.   III. Title: Perfect put-downs and instant
insults.
PN6231.I65R567 1988   88-11710
818'.5402—dc19   CIP
                                                            AC

A Special Willowisp Press, Inc. Edition

Copyright © 1988 by Joseph Rosenbloom
Published by Sterling Publishing Co., Inc.
Two Park Avenue, New York, N.Y. 10016
Manufactured in the United States of America
All rights reserved

10 9 8 7 6 5 4 3 2

Contents

• 1 •
FACING THE MUSIC

Hello, there—tall, dark and obnoxious!

"I just flew in from Europe."
  "They kicked you out that hard?"

You've really got "It"—what, I couldn't say!

I'd like to see you again—but not in person.

What you lack in modesty, you make up for in conceit.

"I'm affected?—*Moi?*"

Your nose is so high in the air—every time you sneeze, you spray the ceiling.

You must have trouble finding hats to fit your head. They don't make them that large.

You have such a swelled head, you have to pin back your ears to get through revolving doors.

You have a great voice. It grates on everyone.

Your singing reminds me of a baseball pitcher who can't throw the ball—off pitch.

I like the way you sing except for two things—my ears.

The only time your voice sounds good is when you gargle.

You sound good when you sing solo—solo no one can hear you.

"Please sing the scale."
    "Do-re-mi-fa-so-la-do."
"You left out the ti."
    "I can't help it. Every time I try to hit a high note, my voice sinks."
    "Again you left out the 't'."

I wish you'd sing Christmas carols. Then I'd only have to listen to you once a year.

You're always forgetting things. You're for getting this, for getting that. . . .

"I wish you were on TV. Then I could turn you off."

"You remind me of the ocean."
   "Because I'm wild and romantic?"
"No, because you make me sick."

You're the kind of person who wants his cake—and everyone else's, too.

Do you realize that every time you breathe, ten people in the world die? Why don't you use mouthwash?

"When tourists visit your town, they go out of their way to see you."
"Because I'm so famous?"
"No, because you're such a sight."

Is that your hair—or did you just walk through a car wash?

You have so many things on your mind, you don't have any room for brains.

Where did you get your brains—at the bird store?

You Remind Me—

You remind me of ice cream—because you're cold, hard and fruity.

You remind me of fleas—because you're always bugging people.

You remind me of the letter T—because you're always starting trouble and finishing last.

You remind me of a chocolate bar—because you're half nuts.

You remind me of an unframed picture—off the wall.

You remind me of a sightseeing boat in Paris—completely in Seine (insane).

You remind me of arithmetic: you add trouble, subtract pleasure, divide attention and multiply ignorance.

Your jokes are so funny—they're greeted by tremendous bursts of silence.

The only funny lines you have are in your face.

Some people are has beens. You're a never was.

You started on the bottom—and it's been downhill ever since.

That was a popular song—at least, it was until you sang it.

Listen to that voice! You sound like a frog with a man in its throat.

Your voice is like asthma set to music.

You sing like a bird—a screech owl!

Your tongue may be sharp, but your voice is flat.

You have a fine voice. Don't spoil it by singing.

You say you can't sing because you have a hoarse throat? Well, why don't you let the horse sing? It probably has a better voice.

If baloney were snow, you'd be a blizzard.

You don't have a better idea—just a louder voice.

"I played Beethoven yesterday."
   "Who won?"

You're always willing to face the music—so long as you can call the tune.

You're so boring, you couldn't even entertain a doubt.

Do you mind if I have you X-rayed? I want to see what you see in you.

I'VE SEEN BETTER—

You've seen better what?

I've seen better hair on coconuts.

I've seen better heads on matches.

I've seen better necks on bottles.

I've seen better tongues on sneakers.

I've seen better bodies on trucks.

I've seen better thighs on chickens.

I've seen better legs on pianos.

Your name must be "Soft Drink," because you'll go out with anyone from 7-Up.

You're so boring that when you go to the beach, the tide refuses to come in.

Your ears are cute. Too bad there's nothing in between.

I don't mind that you're talking, so long as you don't mind that I'm not listening.

Keep talking. I always yawn when I'm interested.

You're so sick, anyone who goes out with you needs a doctor's prescription.

You're so unpopular, you couldn't take out the garbage.

Knock-Knock.
  Who's there?
Celeste.
  Celeste who?
Celeste time I saw
someone with a face like
yours, I threw it a fish.

Knock-Knock.
  Who's there?
Java.
  Java who?
Java great head on your
shoulders. Too bad it's not
on your neck.

Knock-Knock.
  Who's there?
Mustard bean.
  Mustard bean who?
You mustard bean a big
surprise to your parents.
They expected a boy or a
girl.

Knock-Knock.
  Who's there?
Czar.
  Czar who?
Czar all kinds of people in
the world. Too bad you're
not one of them.

Just Because—

Just because you're all wrapped up in yourself doesn't make you a prize package.

Just because you step all over people doesn't mean you're getting up in the world.

Just because you have legs like a canary doesn't mean you're a singer.

Just because you're a million years old and gassy doesn't make you a star.

Just because you go from the frying pan into the fire doesn't make you hot stuff.

Just because your head is shaped like a hubcap doesn't make you a big wheel.

Just because you're a son of a gun doesn't make you a big shot.

Some day you're going to find yourself—and wish you hadn't.

I heard you were going to have your face lifted. But I couldn't figure out who would want to steal it.

You may be beautiful from head to foot—but you're a total mess in between.

People clap when they see you—their hands over their eyes!

You're a real Don Juan—and I Don Juan (don't want) to have anything to do with you.

You have lovely blond hair down your back. It would look better on your head.

My name is Cliff. Why don't you drop over sometime?

· 2 ·
WHAT'S
COOKING?

You are the garlic in the breath of life.

Whatever is eating you must be suffering horribly.

A girl had two dollars for lunch. She bought a bottle of soda for 75 cents, a bag of potato chips for 50 cents, but she still needed a sandwich. Cream cheese and jelly was 80 cents, egg was 90 cents and baloney was 70 cents. What kind of sandwich did she get?
Baloney, just like you're getting.

How dumb am I?

You're so dumb, you would try to shake hands with a palm tree.

You're so dumb, you think the Kentucky Derby is a hat.

You're so dumb, if you went to buy a color TV set, you wouldn't know what color to get.

You're so dumb, I hear you took your nose apart to find out what made it run.

You're so dumb, I hear you put your watch in the piggy bank so you could save time.

Some say you are dead when your brain stops working. They're wrong. Your brain hasn't worked for years.

"Your mind is so low—"
  "How low is it?"
"Your mind is so low that when you get a headache, you put the aspirin in your socks."

Until you came along, I never saw a prune with legs.

The only exercise you get is running people down, sidestepping responsibilities and putting your foot in your mouth.

YOU ARE WHAT YOU EAT—

You are what you eat—you must eat a lot of crumbs.

You are what you eat—you must eat a lot of nuts.

You are what you eat—you must eat a lot of garbage.

You are what you eat—you must eat a lot of spaghetti—you're such a meatball!

THE ONLY REGULAR EXERCISE YOU GET—

The only regular exercise you get is dragging your heels.

The only regular exercise you get is pushing your luck.

The only regular exercise you get is going downhill fast.

The only regular exercise you get is fishing for compliments.

The only regular exercise you get is stepping out.

The only regular exercise you get is driving me crazy.

The only regular exercise you get is running out of nachos.

You're so fat, you can only play Seek.

Why don't you go to the library and brush up on your ignorance?

"My nose is always stuck in a book."
"Right—you're too cheap to buy a bookmark!"

"I've got a mind of my own."
"Good, do you think you can figure out where you left it?"

"I've changed my mind."
"Wonderful—what did you do with the diaper?"

"I've got one of those rare minds—"
"True—it rarely works."

The bigness of your mouth can't hide the smallness of your brain.

Arguing with you is like trying to blow out a light bulb.

Are you sure you don't work for an aspirin company? You're always giving me a headache.

"I'm very fastidious."
"Right, you're fast and you're hideous."

Knock-Knock.
   Who's there?
Avis.
   Avis who?
Avis at the zoo yesterday,
but I didn't see you. It
must have been feeding
time.

Knock-Knock.
   Who's there?
Jupiter.
   Jupiter who?
Jupiter hurry up or you'll
miss the garbage truck.

Knock-Knock.
   Who's there?
Fu Manchu.
   Fu Manchu who?
Fu Manchu their food the
way you do, you pig!

Knock-Knock.
   Who's there?
Eaton.
   Eaton who?
Eaton out of the garbage
again?

Knock-Knock.
   Who's there?
Diego.
   Diego who?
Diego all over your face.
You're the sloppiest eater I
ever saw!

22

Knock-Knock.
   Who's there?
Doughnut.
   Doughnut who?
Doughnut be so smart.
Remember, you can always
be replaced by a human
being.

Knock-Knock.
   Who's there?
Harvard.
   Harvard who?
Harvard you like a knuckle sandwich?

Knock-Knock.
   Who's there?
Butternut.
   Butternut who?
Butternut come any
closer—I have a sensitive stomach.

Knock-Knock.
   Who's there?
Stepfather.
   Stepfather who?
One stepfather and I'll throw up!

Knock-Knock.
   Who's there?
Knockwurst.
   Knockwurst who?
You knockwurst than
anyone I know.

THEY ALL MUST LOVE YOU—

Who must love me?

Farmers must love you—you're always making a pig of yourself.

Pigs must love you—you're such a ham.

Coffee makers must love you—you're an automatic drip.

Maple trees must love you—you're such a sap.

Bakers must love you—you're such a fruitcake.

Knife sharpeners must love you—you're so dull.

Delicatessen owners must love you—you're the wurst.

YOU OUGHT TO BE—

You ought to be an astronaut. You're no earthly good.

You ought to join the army. You're always shooting your mouth off anyway.

You ought to be a magician. People are always asking you to disappear.

You ought to be a garbage collector. You certainly have the mind for it.

You're a detour on the road of life.

"I think I stripped my gears."
"Oh, is that why you're so shiftless?"

Only your red, bloodshot eyes keep you from being entirely colorless.

You have an inferiority complex, and it is entirely justified.

Some people are bad, but you're an exception—exceptionally bad.

You're not as bad as people say—you're worse.

With the cost of living so high, why do you bother?

If I ever said anything nice about you, please cancel it.

When are you going to the zoo to give your face back to the monkey?

"I feel like a piece of chocolate."
"Well, stick around. If I get hungry I'll bite you."

Your cooking defies gravity. It's as heavy as lead, but it won't go down!

Your cooking warms the heart—actually, it gives people heartburn.

Tell me, what was this before you cooked it?

"I'm going to buy some dog food."
"Oh, are you ready for lunch?"

Do you have to leave so soon?
I was about to poison the tea.

· 3 ·
WHICH ONE IS
THE DUMBBELL?

When you're lifting weights, it's hard to tell which one is the dumbbell.

I'm busy now. Do you mind if I ignore you some other time?

Who am I calling stupid? I don't know— what's your name?

You used to have a decent build before your stomach went in for a career of its own.

You look as fit as a fiddle—a bull fiddle.

Just Because

Just because you have athlete's foot doesn't make you an athlete.

Just because you're teed off all the time doesn't make you a golfer.

Just because you were thrown out at home doesn't make you a baseball player.

Just because you've been left back doesn't make you a football player.

Just because you make a racket doesn't make you a tennis player.

The only thing fast about you is your watch.

I used to think turtles were slow—until I saw you running.

YOU'RE SO LAZY—

How lazy
am I?

You're so lazy, you won't even knit your brows.

You're so lazy, you won't even run water.

You're so lazy, you put carfare in your pajamas so you won't even have to walk in your sleep.

You're so lazy, when you have a cold, even your nose won't run.

You're so lazy, you won't even jump to a conclusion.

The only running you have anything to do with is reruns on TV.

You, a jogger? The only thing that runs around your house is the fence!

YOU'RE IN SUCH BAD SHAPE—

How bad is it?

You're in such bad shape, every morning you bend over and touch your toes—with your stomach.

You're in such bad shape, if you played the piano, the piano would win.

You're in such bad shape, if you ran a bath, you'd come in second.

You're in such bad shape, if you beat an egg, we'd all be surprised.

You're in such bad shape, the only muscles (mussels) you've got are still in the shell.

Did you hear the jokes about your muscles? Never mind—they're a lot of mush.

YOU'RE IN SUCH BAD SHAPE—

How bad is it?

You're in such bad shape, you couldn't even catch your breath.

You're in such bad shape, you couldn't even crack a joke.

You're in such bad shape, when you sit down you look like batter spreading.

You're in such bad shape, when you sip lemonade, you have to hold onto your chair to keep from getting sucked back into the straw.

You're in such bad shape, you couldn't even beat a drum.

What makes you think you're in bad shape— just ignore the buzzards flying overhead!

I'm out of shape? You're jello with a belt!

You're in shape all right—the wrong shape!

When you went to the dude ranch, they renamed it the dud ranch.

When you went to Club Med, they renamed it Club Dead.

Your head reminds me of a bowling ball—it's hard, round and has holes in it.

You remind me of racquetball—off the wall.

Your feet are so big, you don't need skis to go water skiing.

THEY ALL MUST LOVE YOU—

Who must love me?

Bowlers must love you—you have a pin head.

Basketball players must love you—you dribble all over yourself.

Tennis players must love you—they love nothing.

Baseball players must love you—you're always out in left field.

Billiards players must love you—you're always behind the eight-ball.

Balloonists must love you—you're so full of hot air.

Race car drivers must love you—you're always trying to pull a fast one.

Now I know reincarnation is a fact. No one could possibly get as stupid as you are in just one lifetime.

You remind me of Plymouth Rock. You have a shape like a Plymouth and a head like a rock.

You must have been hit on the head with a baseball bat when you were a baby, because you've been off base ever since.

If you have to fall, fall on your head. You can't get hurt that way.

Your mouth is getting too big for your muzzle.

"I'm so strong, I can bend bars!"
   "Sure, chocolate bars."

You're strong as an ox and almost as intelligent.

You're a lost treasure. How I wish you'd stay lost!

• 4 •
YOU MOVED!

I heard you were at the dog show. Who won second prize?

You're pretty as a picture—and you should be hung.

You're certainly shipshape—shaped like a ship.

You waited so long for your dreamboat to come in, your pier collapsed.

You have what it takes—but you've had it so long, it's gone bad.

YOU REMIND ME OF A PLANT—

Why? Because I'm so fresh and healthy?

No, because you're green and you smell.

No, because you stay in bed all day.

No, because you're a vegetable.

No, because you have such a big pot.

No, because you smell like fertilizer.

Your stomach is so big that when you get your shoes shined, you have to take the man's word for it.

You're an all-around person—especially around the middle.

You're so fat, you're the same size whether you stand up or sit down.

You're so round, when you fall down you rock yourself to sleep trying to get up.

You weigh so much, when you get into a rowboat, it becomes a submarine.

Fat? You must have a truck scale in your bathroom.

What time is it when you get on a scale? Time to get a new scale!

THE LAST TIME I SAW SOMETHING LIKE YOU—

The last time I saw something like you, I flushed it down the drain.

The last time I saw something like you, it had a hook in it.

The last time I saw something like you, Colonel Sanders fried it.

The last time I saw something like you, it was crawling out from under a rock.

The last time I saw something like you, it had three shiny leaves and a red stem—and I didn't want to touch that, either.

The last time I saw something like you, I cut it in half and both ends wriggled.

THE LAST TIME I SAW
SOMETHING LIKE YOU—

The last time I saw something like you, I took two aspirins and called the doctor.

The last time I saw something like you, I threw it a bone.

The last time I saw something like you, I checked into the hospital to have my eyes examined.

The last time I saw something like you, the undertaker was embalming it.

The last time I saw something like you, it was swinging from a tree and eating a banana.

The last time I saw something like you, the Sanitation Department was trucking it away.

YOU'RE SUCH A BAD ARTIST—

How bad an
artist
am I?

You're such a bad artist, you couldn't even draw your breath.

You're such a bad artist, you couldn't even draw the curtains.

You're such a bad artist, you couldn't even draw a bath.

You're such a bad artist, you couldn't even draw the shade.

You're such a bad artist, you couldn't even draw a sword.

You're such a bad artist, you couldn't even draw a salary.

You're such a bad artist, you couldn't even draw a card from a deck.

Knock-Knock.
  Who's there?
Picasso.
  Picasso.
Picasso who?
  Picasso you I've got this
terrible headache.

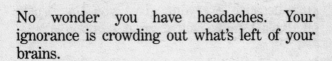

No wonder you have headaches. Your ignorance is crowding out what's left of your brains.

I hear you read a book—once.

Time marches on, why don't you?

You still chase girls—but only downhill.

Of course you're not bald. It's just that the part in your hair covers your whole head.

You once had wavy hair—but one day it waved goodbye.

Greedy? You're a human gimmee pig.

Other than the police, no one is really interested in you.

You ring my chimes. No wonder—you're a real ding-a-ling.

Talent is inherited. For example, Edgar Allan Poe's father used to read Shakespeare. As a result, his son became a great poet. Thomas Edison's father puttered with mechanical things. As a result, his son became a famous inventor. Your father must have fooled around with cuckoo clocks.

Just because everyone gives you the brush off doesn't make you a great painter.

You ought to be a geologist—you have rocks in your head.

You ought to be a geologist—you have so many faults.

"My throat is hoarse."
  "The rest of you looks that way, too."

You have two ears and one tongue, so why don't you listen twice as much as you talk?

You're like a slow leak. People can hear you, but they can't turn you off.

Your mouth reminds me of a car without brakes. It can't be stopped.

You have a waterproof voice. Nothing can drown it out.

You grow on people—like a wart.

You have the manners of a gentleman. Either start using them or give them back!

Your idea of cleaning a room is to sweep it with a glance.

You can help me clean my house. I'd like to mop up the floor with you.

Your home is free of mice and cockroaches. They refuse to live in the same place as you.

You used to be arrogant and obnoxious, but now you're just the opposite. Now you're obnoxious and arrogant.

Your mouth may be fresh, but your ideas are stale.

I can always tell when you're lying—your lips are moving.

You always tell the truth—if it's more convenient.

You always tell the truth—but only after you've run out of lies.

You're a free thinker. Your ideas aren't worth anything.

Anyone who offered you a penny for your thoughts would be overpaying.

"My boyfriend says I'm a peach."
   "That's because you have a heart of stone."

I know an organization that would like to help you—the ASPCA.

If you need me, don't hesitate to ask—someone else!

· 5 ·
COME OUT
FIGHTING!

You may be down to earth, but not far enough down to suit me.

You have a mechanical mind. Too bad all the parts are rusted.

You have a mechanical mind. Too bad the gears are stripped.

You have a mind like half a dictionary—it never gets to "Think."

If you were twice as smart, you'd still be stupid.

How dumb am I?

You're so dumb, the stork that brought you should have been arrested for smuggling dope.

You're so dumb, you would stick your head in a pencil sharpener to sharpen your wits.

You're so dumb, you'd have to go 20,000 fathoms under the sea to have a deep thought.

You're so dumb, you would go to the zoo to look for Christmas seals.

You're so dumb, you would try to wake up sleeping bags.

Of course you don't have an inferiority complex. You're too simple to have any complex.

You're like two tailors who need a bath—a dirty sew-and-sew.

You remind me of a magician who never takes a bath, always up to dirty tricks.

You'll be a great fighter—Your breath would knock anyone out.

Where did you learn to fight—at Kentucky Fried Chicken?

No one can get close to you when you're talking. The blast of hot air drives everyone back.

I wish you'd lose your temper. The one you have now is awful.

When you graduated from school, they gave you a no-class ring.

The only way you can get a hot idea is to stick your head in the oven.

A thought struck you once, and you've been unconscious ever since.

The last time a thought struck you, the experience was so painful, you decided never to let it happen again.

You don't know whether you're coming or going—you must bump into yourself a lot.

Here's a lighted dynamite stick. Please hold it for me till I get back.

Would you mind reaching into your head and getting me a handful of sawdust?

What did your right ear say to your left ear?
  "Do you live on this block, too?"

Your breath is so bad, you have to use industrial strength mouthwash.

You're like a phonograph record. You go round and round, but never get anywhere.

When can you spell idiot in one letter? When it's "U."

"I'm nobody's fool."
"Too bad—maybe somebody will adopt you."

You're the spitting image of your father.
One look at you—and your father spat.

You come from such a crooked family, even your inlaws are outlaws.

You're a square shooter—one of those squares I'd like to shoot.

People like you are like pearls—they need to be strung up.

Knock-Knock.
Who's there?
Juana.
Juana who?
Juana improve your looks?
Wear a mask!

Knock-Knock.
Who's there?
Nanny.
Nanny who?
Nanny your lip!

Knock-Knock.
Who's there?
Raven.
Raven who?
You're a raven maniac!

Knock-Knock.
Who's there?
Quack and Quack.
Quack and Quack who?
Quack another joke like
that and I'll quack you
over the head!

Knock-Knock.
Who's there?
Boyer.
Boyer who?
Boyer not much
in the brain
department!

Knock-Knock.
Who's there?
Ivan.
Ivan who?
Ivan infectious
disease. Please
come closer.

Knock-Knock.
  Who's there?
Frank Lee.
  Frank Lee who?
Frank Lee, your face is
enough to make a rock bleed.

Knock-Knock.
  Who's there?
Olive.
  Olive who?
Olive to sock
you one!

Knock-Knock.
  Who's there?
Goliath.
  Goliath who?
Goliath down—you're
sick in the head.

Knock-Knock.
  Who's there?
Wynott.
  Wynott who?
Wynott leave your brain to
science? Maybe they can
find a cure for it.

Knock-Knock.
  Who's there?
Eureka!
  Eureka who?
Eureka! Why don't
you take a bath?

Knock-Knock.
  Who's there?
Ogre.
  Ogre who?
Ogre take a
flying leap!

"What is frozen water?"
  "Ice."
"What is frozen cream?"
  "Ice cream."
"What is frozen tea?"
  "Iced tea."
"What is frozen ink?"
  "Iced ink."
"Well, why don't you take a bath?"

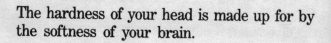

The hardness of your head is made up for by the softness of your brain.

The only thing about you that's on the level is your flat head.

Your head is so flat, flies use it for a landing field.

I could knock the stuffing out of you.
But what would I do with all that sawdust?

If I gave you a towel, would you dry up?

You remind me of a faucet. If only I could turn you off when you acted like a drip.

Do you mind if I ignore you
the rest of my life?

• 6 •
MONKEYING AROUND

I've had a wonderful time—but this isn't it.

I may be a jogger and you may be a jogger, but there's no way I'd ever run around with you.

The only way I'd go around with you is if we were stuck in the same revolving door.

The only way I could be stuck on you is with a stapler.

YOU'RE SO REPULSIVE—

How repulsive am I?

You're so repulsive—even a magnet wouldn't be attracted to you.

You're so repulsive—even the ocean wouldn't wave when it saw you.

You're so repulsive—even a clock wouldn't give you the time of day.

You're so repulsive—even street lights wouldn't turn on when you show up.

You're so repulsive—even a boomerang wouldn't come back to you.

You're so repulsive—even a bee wouldn't buzz you.

You're so repulsive—even an echo wouldn't call you back.

The only kind of kisses you'll ever get from me is the chocolate kind.

The only kind of date you can get is off a calendar.

"At night when I'm asleep, into my dreams you creep. In fact, you're the biggest creep I ever met!"

You have an even disposition—always rotten.

"I feel like a sandwich."
   "Funny, you look more like a marshmallow to me."

You're a real big gun—of small caliber and a big bore.

You have a wonderful face. One look and people wonder.

You have a very striking face. It should be struck more often.

Your face isn't a horror—it's a scream.

Your face looks like mashed potatoes, with the lumps still in them.

If I Gave You—

If I gave you an ax, would you split?

If I gave you a drum, would you beat it?

If I gave you a pogo stick, would you hop it?

If I gave you a rubber band, would you snap out of it?

If I gave you a rope, would you skip it?

If I gave you a parachute, would you drop out?

If I gave you an airline ticket, would you take off?

If I gave you scissors, would you cut out?

If I gave you a scale, would you go weigh?

You don't need luggage when you travel. You have enough bags under your eyes.

Did you hear the joke about your complexion? Never mind, I don't tell off-color stories.

Help reduce air pollution—stop breathing!

I hear you flunked out of dog obedience school. You couldn't keep up with the rest of the class.

If you played hide-and-seek, no one would bother to look for you.

Give you an inch and you think you're a ruler.

THEY ALL MUST LOVE YOU—

Who must love me?

The Invisible Man must love you— you're such a big nothing.

Ghosts must love you—you're such a fright.

Vampires must love you—you're such a pain in the neck.

Mummies must love you—you're so wrapped up in yourself.

Skeletons must love you—you're such a bonehead.

Dracula must love you—you're such a sucker.

Extraterrestrials must love you— you're no earthly good.

THEY ALL MUST LOVE YOU—

Who must love me?

Germs must love you—you're sickening.

Fishermen must love you—you're such a worm.

Scarecrows must love you—you're such a stuffed shirt.

Alarm clocks must love you—you're always ticked off.

Druggists must love you—you're such a pill.

Doctors must love you—your mind is so sick.

Turkeys must love you—the way you fowl up.

You have such a dirty mind, you better shampoo with deodorant.

You remind me of shampoo—the way you're always getting in everyone's hair.

Your head is like a doorknob—anyone can turn it.

You don't wear lipstick. You can't keep your mouth closed long enough to put it on.

You're a very modest person, and you have lots to be modest about.

When I see two people together and one looks bored, the other one is you.

The only polish you have is on your nails.

The only polish you'll ever have is on your shoes.

You're one in a million—thank goodness!

After not seeing you for so long, all I want to say is—so long!

· 7 ·
THE LATEST DOPE

What's the latest dope—besides you?

"And then, thousands of feet up above the ground, I pulled the string. I knew that should my parachute fail to open, I would dash my poor brains out on the ground below."

"And did you?"

The sharpness of your tongue is only exceeded by the dullness of your mind.

You must be a terrible bowler. Your mind is always in the gutter.

"I have a dynamic personality."
   "Yes, and it's underwhelming!"

May I have your picture? I need it for my dart board.

You're so loud, you even whisper at the top of your voice.

You talk twice as fast as anyone can listen.

You remind me of last week's newspaper: stale, unimportant, and filled with bad news.

You have the germ of an idea. Please don't spread it around.

"I passed your house yesterday."
  "Thanks awfully!"

Why do you take yourself so seriously? No one else does.

The only way you'll ever get a fine finish is to drink shellac.

Anyone who told you to be yourself couldn't have given you worse advice.

How much would you charge to haunt a house?

You're such a big nothing, you have to rent a shadow.

You're such a big nothing that when you get into a taxi, the driver keeps the "Vacant" sign up.

I hear the President is going to declare you a national disaster area.

You may go around in circles, but you're still a square.

You've seen better what?

I've seen better teeth on a comb.

I've seen better arms on a chair.

I've seen better faces on clocks.

I've seen better ears on corn.

I've seen better hands on a watch.

I've seen better noses on airplanes.

I've seen better eyes on potatoes.

It's great to have brains. But then again, how would you know?

You have rare ideas. It's rare when you have any.

Once there was a river with a bridge across it. On one side was a banana tree. On the other side was a mother monkey and her baby monkey. They were hungry, so the mother monkey crossed the bridge to the banana tree. But while she was there, the river flooded and wiped out the bridge. Now the question is: how can the little monkey get across the river and join his mother at the banana tree?

Well, if a big monkey like you can't figure it out, how do you expect a little monkey to do it?

There are three kinds of people: those who make things happen, those who watch things happen—and people like you, who wonder what happened.

Knock-Knock.
  Who's there?
Sue.
  Sue who?
Sue-prise me—say
something intelligent.

Knock-Knock.
  Who's there?
Dresden
  Dresden who?
Dresden rags again,
I see.

Knock-Knock.
  Who's there?
Carmen or Cohen.
  Carmen or Cohen who?
You don't know if you're
Carmen or Cohen.

Knock-Knock.
  Who's there?
Alice.
  Alice who?
Alice thought you
were a big zero.

Knock-Knock.
  Who's there?
Hertz.
  Hertz who?
Hertz my eyes just
to look at you.

Knock-Knock.
  Who's there?
Avenue.
  Avenue who?
Avenue thought of checking
into the home for the
chronically strange?

Knock-Knock.
　Who's there?
Juan.
　Juan who?
Juan of these days—
pow!—right
in the kisser!

Knock-Knock.
　Who's there?
Cash.
　Cash who?
I always knew
you were some kind
of nut!

Knock-Knock.
　Who's there?
Harmony.
　Harmony who?
Harmony rocks did they
have to turn up before
they found you?

Knock-Knock.
　Who's there?
Theonie.
　Theonie who?
Theonie trouble
with your face is
that it shows.

Knock-Knock.
　Who's there?
Colin.
　Colin who?
Colin all drugstores!
One of your pills
is missing!

Knock-Knock.
　Who's there?
Desi.
　Desi who?
Desi good reason why you
think the world is against
you—it is!

YOU HAVE SUCH A BIG MOUTH—

How big is it?

You have such a big mouth, when you yawn, your ears disappear.

You have such a big mouth, when you yawn, your pants fall down.

You have such a big mouth, when the dentist asked you to open your mouth wide, he fell in.

You have such a big mouth, you can eat a banana sideways.

You're so full of ignorance, it's coming out of your mouth.

You think you're sharp as a tack, but you're only tacky.

You approach every subject with an open mouth.

Do you know how to improve your speech? Use shortening.

Every time you open your mouth, some idiot starts talking.

I used to think there was no such thing as a perpetual motion machine until I saw your mouth in action.

Even an owl wouldn't give a hoot for you.

Your conversation is so dull, you won't even talk to yourself.

There are two sides to every question—your side and the truth.

That Last Joke...

That last joke of yours was about as funny as a helicopter with an ejection seat.

That last joke of yours was like a bunch of fleas— gone to the dogs.

That last joke of yours was like last week's bread—stale.

That last joke of yours was like chicken feed—strictly for the birds.

That last joke of yours was two-thirds of a pun—PU.

"Did you hear the joke about the moron who kept on saying no?"
"No."
"So you're the one!"

Your jokes are from Poland—they get Warsaw and Warsaw.

The closest you'll ever come to being a joker is to find one in a deck of cards.

You're such a hog, pigs must follow you around!

Do skunks come up to you and ask you how you do it?

Let's play horse. I'll be the front end, and you just be yourself.

Half of your jokes are witty. No wonder you're a half-wit.

I'll never forget the first time I met you— but I'll keep trying.

As the painter said to the wall, "One more crack like that and I'll plaster you?"

I am here with an open mind, a complete lack of prejudice and a cool approach to hear the rubbish you are about to tell me.

People like you who think they know everything are annoying to those of us who do.

You irk me. In fact, you're the biggest irk I know.

Be careful you don't break your arm patting yourself on the back.

You're like the Invisible Man—nothing to look at.

You croak like a frog—and I wish you would!

· 8 ·
PLAYING HOOKY

You're the only person I know who got a D in recess.

You'd be better off if you had more bone in the spine and less in the head.

You're a big pill—hard to take and tough to swallow.

You think you're a big wheel, but you're only a flat tire.

You think you're an actor, but the only thing you can play is hooky.

You're like time off from school: no class.

I know you're not the worst person in the world, but until a worse one comes along—you'll do.

You're in a class by yourself—no wonder, no one wants to sit next to you.

You were different from the other five-year-olds in your kindergarten class. You were twelve.

When you were promoted from kindergarten, you were so excited, you cut yourself shaving.

You were in the same grade so long, people began to think you were the teacher.

It was a great day when you graduated. The teachers cried for joy—they thought they'd never get rid of you.

The only first class thing about you is some of the mail you get.

I can live without air for minutes, without water for days, without food for weeks, and without you—forever!

The world is made up of all kinds of people: the lower crust, the upper crust, and people like you—just crust.

You really use your head—to keep the rain off your neck!

I used to think you were a big pain in the neck. Now I have a much lower opinion of you.

I used to hear ugly rumors about you. Now I know they aren't rumors. You *are* ugly.

If you changed, it would have to be an improvement. You couldn't get any worse.

Your brain is a miracle—it's a miracle when it works!

Everyone has a right to be stupid—but you abuse the privilege.

You couldn't be as stupid as you look. Stupidity doesn't come in that size!

WHEN THEY WERE GIVING OUT—

When they were giving out brains— you thought they said trains—and you've been on the wrong track ever since.

When they were giving out noses—you thought they said roses, and asked for a big red one.

I was going to buy some handkerchiefs for your birthday, but I couldn't find any big enough for your nose.

Your nose is so big, you only have to breathe in once and it lasts all day.

Is that your nose—or are you wearing a tomato?

Is that your nose—or are you minding it for an elephant?

Dracula would turn you down. He wants blood, not crud.

"I'm going to the blood bank."
  "Overdrawn again?"

Before you become a blood donor, make sure you're a blood owner.

In the medical books, where they describe a moron, they mention you as a perfect example.

No one can resist you. Your breath is enough to make anyone cave in.

You Remind Me—

You remind me of a tiny deck of cards: you're no big deal.

You remind me of a school without a head: you lack principles.

You remind me of a school without teachers: you've lost your faculties.

You remind me of a movie star—Boris Karloff.

You remind me of an old pair of shoes—a lowdown heel with no sole.

You remind me of a whale—always spouting off.

You remind me of a flower—you lilac crazy.

You remind me of a canoe—you behave better when paddled from the rear.

You Remind Me—

You remind me of a broom: anyone can shove you around.

You remind me of a movie star— Lassie.

You remind me of an amoeba—you're a lower form of life.

You remind me of a postage stamp— anyone can lick you.

You remind me of oil out of the ground: crude, greasy and unrefined.

You remind me of oatmeal—lukewarm and mushy.

You remind me of a watermelon— pitiful.

You remind me of a yo-yo—you're such a jerk.

"How many ribs are there on a jackass?"
  "Open your shirt and we'll find out."

"How many hairs are there on a pig's head?"
  "Next time you use a comb, count them."

"How many toes are on a monkey's foot?"
  "Take off your shoes and let's see."

When you say, "I'm a monkey's uncle!", you must be talking about your family.

Your mouth is like a chicken—foul!

I've heard of large chickens, but you're the biggest cluck I've ever seen!

There's a bus leaving in five minutes. Why don't you get under it?

· 9 ·
WHERE HAVE YOU BEEN ALL MY LIFE?

Where have I been all your life? Mostly avoiding you.

Have you seen me someplace before? It's possible. I've been someplace before.

Have you seen me someplace else? Yes—and how I wish I were there now.

I'd like to have the pleasure of this dance, so please dance with someone else.

THE ONLY TIME

The only time you have a heart is when you're playing cards.

The only time you have charms is when you wear a bracelet.

The only time you have appeal is when you're eating a banana.

You're so cold-blooded, if Dracula bit you he'd get pneumonia.

I think of your personality several times every day—each time I open the refrigerator.

You not only don't know what's up—you don't know what's down or sideways.

You must have gotten up on the wrong side of your cage this morning.

"You're such a pretty girl."

"Thanks. Of course you'd say that, even if you didn't think it."

"Of course, and you'd think it even if I didn't say it."

It was love at first sight. Then I took another look.

I see you're dressing formally today. You're wearing a clean shirt.

The only time you wash your ears is when you eat watermelon.

THEY ALL MUST LOVE YOU—

Who must love me?

Squirrels must love you—you're such a big nut.

Caterpillars must love you—you're such a total creep.

Fishes must love you—you're all wet.

Owls must love you—you never give a hoot.

Pet owners must love you—you've gone to the dogs.

Cats must love you—you have such a funny puss.

Cows must love you—you're so moo-dy.

Snowmen must love you—you're so flaky.

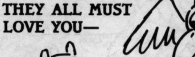

THEY ALL MUST LOVE YOU—

Who must love me?

Lawyers must love you—you're such a case.

Ventriloquists must love you—you're such a dummy.

Birdwatchers must love you—you're so featherbrained.

Brooks must love you—you never stop babbling.

Eye doctors must love you—you're always making a spectacle of yourself.

Soldiers must love you—you're always shooting your mouth off.

Toreadors must love you—you're so full of bull.

Comedians must love you—you're such a joke.

Just Because

Just because you have a short fuse doesn't make you dynamite.

Just because you're always flying off the handle doesn't make you a pilot.

Just because you can switch on an electric light doesn't make you a live wire.

Just because your head comes to a point doesn't make you real sharp.

Just because your nose runs a lot doesn't make you a jogger.

There was something about you I liked, but you spent it.

You believe in give-and-take relationships— so long as I'm the one that gives and you're the one that takes.

If your dress were any shorter, it would be a collar.

If your dress were cut any lower, you wouldn't need socks.

You're like sugar—pale, lumpy and shapeless.

You have quite a figure. No one can quite figure it out.

You're dark and handsome. The darker it is, the handsomer you look.

You have what it takes. Better give it back before the police catch up with you.

The only place you can dig up a date is in the cemetery.

When the phone rings, people hope it isn't you.

You've been turned down more often than a bed.

I don't mind you hanging around my house. I just don't want you coming inside.

You're so full of hot air, you have to be careful not to start forest fires by breathing the wrong way.

You could put out forest fires all by yourself. You're a total wet blanket.

Why Don't You Make Like—

Why don't you make like an insect and bug off?

Why don't you make like a boat and shove off?

Why don't you make like the wind and blow?

Why don't you make like a curtain and pull yourself together?

Why don't you make like a rocket and blast off?

Why don't you make like an actor and bow out?

Why don't you make like an egg and get cracking?

All you have to do to lose ten pounds is to take a bath.

Your idea of an exciting evening is a sight-seeing trip through a garbage dump.

Your idea of an exciting evening is to turn up the electric blanket.

You looked everywhere and finally found someone worthy of your love—you!

You're the salt of the earth. No wonder your kisses taste so awful.

Haven't you ever wondered why people close their eyes when they kiss you?

"I'd go to the ends of the earth for you."
  "Yes—but would you stay there?"

I would die for you, but mine is an undying love.

How can I leave you? By bus, taxi, subway, airplane or on foot.

Don't go away mad—just go away!

· 10 ·
MOTHER NATURE'S BIGGEST MISTAKE

How is Mother Nature's biggest mistake today?

"That man is following me. I think he's crazy."
"I think so, too."

There are three sexes: male, female—and you.

A day without you is like a day with sunshine.

You look like lemon tastes.

"I'm unattached."
    "No, I think you're just put together sloppily."

You spend so much time hunting for food in the refrigerator, your nose suffers from frostbite.

"I went to beauty school."
    "Couldn't pass the physical?"

"I went to charm school."
    "Flunked out?"

I don't think you're pretty and I don't think you're ugly. I think you're pretty ugly.

"You look like a million dollars."
    "Don't kid me. You never saw a million dollars."
    "You're right. You look like nothing I ever saw."

You may be a beautiful person on the inside. Too bad it's the outside that shows.

Would you like to see what a creature from outer space looks like? Here's a mirror.

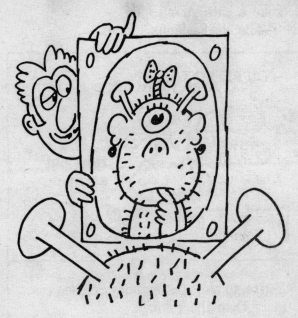

Your face reminds me of a relief map. It's a relief when I don't have to look at it.

If it weren't for your pot belly, you'd have no shape at all.

You went on a crash diet? No wonder you look like such a wreck!

Of course, you're not fat—you're just tall around the waist!

"You look like a cross between Oliver Twist and David Copperfield."

"Like a cute young kid?"

"No—like the Dickens."

YOU'RE SO OLD—

How old am I?

You're so old, the birthday candles cost more than the cake.

You're so old, by the time you light the last birthday candles, the first ones are out.

You're so old that when you went to school, history was current events.

Old? There were so many candles on your birthday cake, the ceiling was barbecued!

"My hands are soft because I wear gloves at night."

"You must also sleep with a hat on."

The way you dress, you could enter the Mess America contest.

This is the first time I've seen a burlap bag with sleeves.

Your clothing fits like a glove. It sticks out in five places.

You're a regular clotheshorse. Your clothing would look better on a horse.

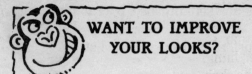

WANT TO IMPROVE YOUR LOOKS?

Want to improve your looks?
Walk backwards.

Want to improve your looks?
Pay someone normal to say he's you.

Want to improve your looks?
Wear a hat—right over your face.

You should wear a sign on your head: HELP WANTED.

If you went to a mind reader, you'd get your money back.

You may be slow-witted, but you're fast-tongued.

The only way you can make up your mind is to put lipstick on your forehead.

I hope you have unemployment insurance for your brain. It hasn't worked since I've known you.

There is a cure for your lack of brains. It's called "silence."